# UNFINISHED YET WHOLE

# Unfinished Yet Whole

Reyana Joy

# Contents

To the One who first told me
I had a story to write and then proceeded
to write it through me.

To my dear readers,

This book is a journey. A journey I took through the end of high school and the transition to college. Each part is a section I organized to chronologically show how God was working during that season of my life. I want you to follow that story with me, to learn along the way like I did, to see the realizations, the heartbreak, the getting-back-up-again, the restoration. No matter if it takes you a day or years to finish this journey, I invite you to take the time to soak it all in.

God wrote this story through me these past few years, and I believe His purpose was for me to share it. Each poem has the potential to touch someone's heart and to relate to someone's story. I hope you find the one that speaks to you in louder, more blaring volumes, the one that wrecks your heart, only to put it back together again.

I give you permission to scribble all over this book. Write in the margins. Underline or circle words. Scratch notes about where you were, the date you read it, or how it spoke to you. This book is not only a journey, but it is a *journal* for you to record your dreams and struggles and the things weighing you down and fears and loves and your own poems and your own stories and the things you never said out loud. This is a safe place.

More than anything, I hope you can feel God in these poems because it was Him writing through me. I don't believe I am naturally able to articulate my thoughts in this way, yet His hand guided my pen on those tear-filled nights when I couldn't speak and couldn't pray. In all of this, the biggest lesson I have learned is that He is not finished with me. He is not finished with you. We are unfinished, and we still get to put pen to paper. He still grants us permission to write down these things.

And *yet,* we are whole because of Jesus. God, by His grace, sent His Son to die on that cross for our sins. His blood has taken our broken pieces, our shattered bodies, and pieced them together again to make something brilliant, something beautiful, something beyond.

Take this time to go on a journey with yourself, and if you'd like, invite God to come with you and guide you. You'll never know what He is trying to speak to you until you take the time to *listen.*

With love,

Reyana Joy

# I

## what came before

## WHAT DO THESE THINGS TELL YOU?

where do all the leaves
normally go?

this morning, i strolled past
the brick building of my high school

and could actually see the
color of the ground,

rainy cement, and even though
it was desolate,

there was beauty in
its barrenness.

leaves were piled up
in the corners on sidewalks

with green and brown and red,
puddles from a late rain,

and later, i saw a clothesline
shaped like a cross.

## DISCOVERED

on a busride leaving chicago,
i asked this boy what
his hopes and dreams were.
his eyes grew wide,
but then he answered,
almost unfazed,
and i think deep down
people want to be discovered.

## GUARDED

i guard my heart.
i keep my secrets
locked away.
if there's no chance
you'll love me,
then i won't bother
to stay.

## THE ANGER YOU DON'T KNOW ABOUT

a flame formed in my heart full
of sawdust i left just for you to burn,
because i never believed
you'd actually see
me through.

i tried to forget
the dizzy numb feeling of
your fingers forming the braid,
tying my heart together
in places i would have to
untangle later.

it was six a.m. and our eyes
had not found sleep.
whispers in the dark,
i found a place for my head to rest
on the divot of your heart
beating in your chest.

but it all changed on a short van ride
to a place called home, but the home
we found together could never be so.
i buried the anger that settled in my soul
so your future self would never have to know.

## THE REASON I LEFT

you were so kind,
so gentle.
the predictable tide that
kept drawing in

and touching my sandy toes
to clean them once again.
but you weren't the waves.
you weren't the storms.

i think walking down that tide
gave me some time to think,
to realize. i think my heart loved
your steady, consistent beat

and would have passed the world by
just to stay for one more hug.
but then i left you for a rhythm
of seas that might churn my soul.

i think my heart was somewhere
yours could not travel to.
and sometimes i wonder:
*how bad of a storm did i cause in you?*

## LIKE SALT—YOU DISSOLVED

you've changed.
      there's something about you
that started to use a butterfly net
      to catch the cares of the world
instead of the longings
      of your soul.
parts of you have faded away
      like how dandelions disappear
as the summer turns to fall.
      you're scared of the silence
because you no longer
      have words to fill it.
where is your soul?
      maybe i can find it
where you lost it
      and return it
to you.

I ONCE WAS LOST

you found me
broken and afraid in a pile of
dried sand in the desert,
thirsty, hungry,
in need of protection
and love.

you found me
wandering through fields and fields
of fading flowers,
trying to see which one would
take me into a land called Forever.

you found me
curled in my own arms
full of tears and hurt,
crying out for your help,
even when i'd given you none of me,
expecting your love to fall down on me,
to pick me up,
and then hoping you would still
carry me home.

you found me
drowning in my own flesh,
my limbs failing me,
and you pulled my soul
right out of the water
and said,
*"i'm always here to save you."*

## WHERE DID WE GO WRONG?

from a young age,
we learn to draw smiley faces
on cold windows where the precipitation
has reached our side.

but as we grow older,
we start to paint the smiles
onto  o u r s e l v e s
even though the frigid outside world

has come to haunt us.
there's nothing to smile about here.
yet we hide behind a window
with the face a child drew.

## TO THE BOY I ONCE LOVED

my words sliced you open
the way an apple peeler leaves only
the tender part behind,                    yes,
you were mine.

the seeds in your heart grew
but they never fully found
their roots established or                 entwined.
and i think the idea of a tree

growing here was just majestic
enough for me to hold on
a bit longer—even though it was            breaking
you inside.

i'm sorry for the hurt
i caused you. i hope the growing
was worth it and that                      someday
some girl will see the pain

i formed in you
and help you to find
a place to sustain the wilted              roots
i left behind.

## TIME NOT TO MYSELF

my first day at home with actual time that
i'm not cramming in like a suitcase,
and yet it still seems to fall over.

i don't do my hair,
i just run my hands through it
and think of him
because that's the sort of thing
we talk about.

i'm wearing the sweatshirt i wore
last time i saw him,
and i wish his scent still hung
on the sleeves,
but now it feels like a washed up memory
of the last time we laughed.

the other night on the phone,          (221 minutes)
he told me my hair was beautiful,
while i couldn't stop playing with the ends.
he read the card back to me and promised
he liked the real me no matter what.

my mind is not as blank
as it used to be.

## ANOTHER BATTLE LOST

it's the same everyday.
i'm starting to turn into them.
my smiles are gone,
and people wonder what happened.
i can't explain it
because i don't know either.
except that this world is
ripping me to pieces.
the blows keep finding my gut,
and they leave with them the same
sour taste of you're not good enough.

i keep waving my white flag,
but no one seems to see.
somewhere along the way
my armor got loose
and started to drag.
      drag
      me
      down.
please help me
find my sword.
i can't lift it
anymore.

## I KEEP TELLING MYSELF

i wasn't prepared.
my memories tangle sheets,
and i have no more control
once my feet hit the floor.
the sound of waves
sabotages my days
and nothing makes sense.
so many times
i tell myself,
"if this happens,
i'll break."

and it happened.
yet somehow,
i still wake up
every morning,
my feet meeting the floor
and a tornado swirls me up,
twisting my body
into so much terror
that i sink down and cry
that nothing has changed today.

## HOLDING ON AND LETTING GO

i had a dream last night
that i hugged you,
but when i woke up,
i realized that is no more.

i know it's for the best,
it's just hard to let you go
when i was trying to hold on
so tight the grip left scars.

you let go of your rope,
but i'm still standing here
trying to let it fall
from my grasp.

please don't come back.
i'm doing all i can
to forget those nights
and find myself again.

## OLD POEMS I NEVER WROTE DOWN—
## I WAS TOO LATE

you thanked me once
for giving you a chance.
it's been hard,
but i keep reminding myself
why i did,
and why i still do.
i guess i'll keep giving them to you
until either you don't want me to
or i've run out.

/ / /

i'm holding
all these little moments
so close because i'm worried
there won't be any more.
sometimes,
i can't remember
what you sound like,
and you feel like an imaginary boy
i painted in my head.
everything about you
seems like a dream.

/ / /

it was hard at first.
but i learned how to live without you.
i'd done it for so long already.

## LONG LOST

yes, my heart grew
      o l d
and
      t i r
         e
           d
this winter.
where have you
                been?

## MEETING OUR SAVIOR

we drift through life
not looking for His love,
but somehow
He finds us
w a n d e r i n g,
finds us
s e a r c h i n g,
finds us

        hopelessly trying
          to climb a

            n  t
         u       a
       o          i
     m             n

       that isn't our home,
and there He takes us back
and reminds us
what it is like
to be loved.

## BROKEN PROMISES

i'm sorry if he broke your heart
or if she turned her back on you.
you need to remember humans
are imperfect,
and the promises they make
can break easily too.
some are more loyal than others,
but if a promise is shattered,
you can still pick it up from the ground
and give it back.
you are stronger now
without it holding you down.

# FRAIL: A FRAGILE TRUE STORY

she liked seeing her
concaving stomach and sharp,
breathless ribs.

people asked what was wrong,
but she just felt sick.
> *i can't eat much yet.*

she couldn't admit it
to that woman who saw right through
her skeleton eyes.

all she thought about was food—
how much she wanted it,
> but also how much she wanted
> to stay away from it.

she could only see the extra pounds
she wanted to extinguish.
> *they told me i had big ears and a big nose.*

/ / /

she left for a clinic
where most stay three weeks.
> she was there two months.

they watched her every move,
her bathroom breaks,
her resting heart rate of 40 beats,

her every calorie eaten,
sometimes more than 4,000 a day.
> *my dad just told me to eat.*

21

all the girls at the clinic relapsed.
      and one even died.
but eventually, she found her way home.

*she* survived.

## TO THE BOY OR GIRL WHO STRUGGLES WITH SUICIDAL THOUGHTS:

you're scared.
scared of what might happen to you
when no one is around,
when you are all alone,
all alone with those nasty,
      corrupt,
terrifying thoughts
you can't seem to get rid of.
you don't want to die—
yet you think it's the only way
to end this agony,
this everyday hell.

when will it stop?

you want to ask for help,
but the word "suicidal"
can't form on your lips.
you think it's just a phase.
your thoughts will stop,
won't they?
thoughts have ways of making
permanent paths.
the engraved road there is
life-altering destruction.

but luckily the Creator
of you and me
made a path to light and love
that doesn't exist without Him.
you see, He had to let the nail
pierce *through* His hand,
to touch the light on the other side,
to pierce the darkness,
and to eventually come back out again,

leaving a hole that brings light to shadows.
a painful space revealed and created
for sinners to enter in.
light needed to be
shining through
the other side.
He did this for me.
He did this for you.

poke your finger in this hole.
He wants you to enter.
to see the light He has provided
through the grief of a painstaking death
so that you would have life.
hold onto it now.
He has provided a way.

## THIS IS FOR YOU

you can do it.
it doesn't need to
control your life.
there is so much more to you.
the way you make paper airplanes backwards
or always double-knot your shoes.
the way you wake up and immediately make your bed
or hum as you brush your hair.
the way you trace your fingers
over the same chip in the doorway
or how you hold yourself when you cry.
there's so much to you,
so much that you are stronger,
stronger than you think.

## THERE'S SO MUCH LIFE TO LIVE

there's so many more moments,
like the first time you enter
your new house
with the squeaky door
and mud on the floor
or the way you feel after painting
a whole room to yourself,
sweat dripping from your brow
but the ache in your muscles reminding you
of the work you accomplished.

there's so many more
songs to hum,
suckers to lick,
children to tickle,
hands to hold,
lightning bugs to catch,
snowflakes to chase,
and christmas trees to decorate.

remember,
your life is not over yet.
each day is full
of so
       many
           moments.

don't blow them all away.

## TRENCH WARFARE

i've been sitting in the mud
of these man-made trenches too long.
they are *protection* we tell ourselves,
but everyday i'm here
takes a piece of my soul
and sinks it into the mud and mire.
these trenches we dug cover ourselves
from the enemy lines,
but isn't the enemy the one who hides
instead of showing love?
we have become our own enemies here.

trench warfare has consumed
our lives.
we are complacent,
sitting in this mud,
shooting at something we can't see,
waiting, barely feeling anything,
that's how long it takes,
our hearts growing numb.
when will we take the risk
and go out into no-mans land,
where few have dared to go?

fear of barbed wire and gunshots,
my boots sink deeper in the
holes of mud we dug.
but the Lord is with me.
i can confidently go into this battle.
this trench doesn't define me.
Jesus Christ does that.
i don't ever want to go back.
i don't ever want to hide behind
that man-made trench,

thinking of excuses and
sinking in fear as
it drowns my soul,
and soon the mustard gas will come,
and i'll have no place to go.
i want to run after Jesus,
through the fire.
and if they shoot at me,
Lord, i pray the bullets

will pierce my body,
but never my soul.
i'd rather go down giving you glory
and spreading your name
than go down a coward
who never buried their fear.
Lord, you carry me through
this dark path man has made,
and you promise to be with me always.
my heart has left the trenches and
the only thing protecting me
is you.

# II

how it happened

## WOUNDS INTO WORDS

i lay in a sobbing mess
on my bedroom floor.
my weight is shifting like
the sand carried away on the beach,
and my hair is splayed out
like the kindergarten drawings
on the playground.

but you see me here
and pick me up to brush me off.
those tears,
they'll heal.
you turn my wounds
into words,
right here,
on this page.

## QUARANTINED

stuck in my home
and my two scandinavian sisters
have left for europe.
time is a strange, slow-moving thing,
yet when the sun starts to set,
a whole day has gone past,
and i want time to come back.

i haven't had this much time to myself
since the summer i was twelve.
how do i fill this space
with the ticking of the clock
ringing in my ears and
reminding me
that i am going
nowhere
yet passing through an infinite
amount of time?

i am scared to move forward.

## WHAT IT'S LIKE BEING A PEOPLE-PLEASER

you are walking around walls
you didn't build,
trying to navigate where *not* to go
and where you can travel no further.
you try smiling and laughing at things
that aren't funny.
a compliment?
how about two?
you only say something about yourself
if they ask. make sure they're pleased
in your company. the worst is if they aren't,
and you can't do anything to fix it.

these walls you walk around are always
                              confining,
              draining,
suffocating.
you're locked in with your fake smiles.

when will you
break down their walls?
ask them things
they weren't expecting.
don't dance around the truth,
go straight for it.
what do you have to lose?

*people pleasing punched me*
*in the gut, and i'm looking both ways*
*for cars that never come.*

## WHEN GOING NOWHERE

it is dry here
in this land
of uncertainty.
people aren't seeing
that spring is on its way.
we are stuck
in nowhere.

yet i hold onto the hope
that someday i will give
my children this,
this proof that i was here,
here in nowhere,
wherever that was,
nowhere to be found.

*dear daughter,*
*i pray that you know*
*your Creator loves you*
*whether your blossom is blooming*
*or the rain has blown*
*your leaves away.*

*dear son,*
*i pray that you know*
*your emotions and passions*
*are beautiful because your Father in Heaven*
*made you to think this way.*

i'm praying for the day
when i will hold my babies,
and even if i am still in the land
of nowhere,
they will have proof that i was here,
here on this page.

and that even before they existed,
they will know that
they were in the land of nowhere
with me too.

# I AM LEARNING

the problems that aren't
so bad yet still

        s t i n g

to the touch,
and they tell you
they aren't

           w o r t h y,

and you are worthless
in your

       w o r r y.

in truth,
she told me
they weren't

          n o t h i n g.

if i was worried,
that was

       s o m e t h i n g.

## DRY BONES AND A DUSTY TEAPOT

there's a girl out there
who jumps up and down
at the sound of
dry bones rattling.

there's a girl who aches
from the lies of the world
and how they lead people
        a s t r a y.

there's a girl who carries a hurting heart
that is almost going to break,
who often feels tired and that
there is nothing left.

yesterday, her words
moved me to break the lies
that this dusty teapot
was no good,
and she gave me permission
to bring it to the table
and pour her a cup of something
i've been brewing too long.

this girl carries the world,
and it often breaks her.
but God is walking so close,
He always catches her.

## MY COLLECTION

i collect extra replacement buttons
meant for shirts and keep them
in my desk, along with
my safety pins and paper clips.
the kind that get forgotten,
never to fulfill their purpose,
lost somewhere in nowhere.

i collect extra words
that came out wrong and
somehow manage to stab me
in the throat and those
go right next to all
the thoughts i want to scream out,
but somehow,
they never reach my mouth.

i collect extra tears
when the world is crying
after being dry and numb
for a while,
or from the fact
that there is finally a crack
dripping from
the constant weight.

those tears are collected
in a broken bottle
that never leaks,
and my organized mess breaks,
but instead of hiding it
in my drawer,
i set the extra button
by the bottle of tears.

someday, i will catch up
with all the years
that have snagged my sweaters
and drawn buckets from the water-wells.
yes, someday those buttons and words
will be worth something next to
my bottle of tears.

## WHAT I SAW TODAY IN THE WORLD

driving with mom,
listening to a sermon,
seeing trash bags on trees
like chewed gum.

here's to the woman
who is still out in that garden,
despite the wind and the work,
she is appreciated.
i hope she knows.
through the dirt and the muck
with our backs sore and our knees stuck,
we keep working
to make something
we believe in.

let us not give up
despite the world swirling
around us.
we pick up one more seed,
dig one more hole,
cover it up again.
there is beauty when
we push through the thorns and thistles
to get to the growing flowers.

CULTIVATING BLESSINGS

Jesus,
who am i that you would
bless me with this wind?
i am grateful, even here.
with a tree that bends at
your command,
with new growth of leaves and branches
and grass that is finally green again.
a flat skyline
with cultivated farms,
bright with hope of springtime
and their soil filled with seeds.
your seeds, Lord.
i am here to plant your seeds
in a field of possibility.
someday,
they will grow to the sky where we all
like to imagine you are.
but it's even more beautiful than that.
because you are right here.
ever with us.

## I PRAY TODAY

i pray that today
you will let your hair
blow over your face
and not brush it away.

i pray that you will gain the courage to
write the words
nestled and tucked away
in your heart.

i pray that you will
watch the sun fall and
let it kiss you on
its way out.

i pray that you know
how loved you
really are.

i pray as the wind gives you goosebumps
and you watch the stars come out,
that you feel the Father holding you.

you are safe in this place.

# WAKING UP THE WORLD

driving for the first time
in two weeks felt strange.
of course, the highways
in this little corner of nebraska
weren't filled more than usual,
and the streets and houses
still seemed empty as i drove through,
like a whisper could sneak in between
and still be heard.
this quiet, dusty town felt almost abandoned
like a wartorn village
with the yellowing welcome sign
and dirt lawns for landscape.
but as i drove,
i saw glimmers of hope
in a pink blossoming tree
outside a torn-down house,
barely able to survive.
yet the tree grew
among the mess,
and i believe that we,
as human beings,
would
as well.

## WATCHING SUNSETS WITH THE GIRL
## WHO CARRIES STARS IN HER POCKETS

leaving supper early,
catching the sunset before it falls down
on the ocean,
a bridge and bare feet over a
swampy grassland overlooking the bay,
praising the Creator,
pink hues and prayers,
a woman and her dog,
laughter on the pier,
our hearts poured out in tears.
               *"just wait, it only gets better."*
with sticky sweaty skin
and bugs that cling,
we watch as pink paints the sky
and soon the moon is visible
and the stars break through.

now as i remember this,
i really miss you.

## UNREQUITED LOVE

it's the reason i cried
over a breakup
before it even started.

it's the reason i had
doubts about how good
of a friend i was
with friends who had done
so much for me and loved me,
even for a short time.
was i enough for them?

it's the reason i was so afraid
you had been mad at me
this whole time.
i hadn't recognized your love
because i was consumed
with doubt.

> (my hands sweat
> as i write this.)

to the friends who have taken the time
to see my brokenness, to see past the surface
of this perfectionism
i try to display.
thank you for sticking true.
i still have fears
of losing you.

but i realize,
God loved me
even before i knew Him.
He is the King of loving people
who don't love Him back.

*Jesus,*
*i'm sorry when i*
*turned my back on you.*

maybe i can love
the unlovable too.
maybe i can still
give my all to people
even if they leave me.
maybe i was put here
to love the people you placed
in my path.

i shouldn't fear love.
because Jesus first loved me.

## I AM CAUGHT

Lord, you say you love me
and delight in me even in my
struggle,
but sometimes i let
my doubt flood me
like the ocean, and
i'm trying to hold
onto the pier so
i don't drown,
and just when i'm
about to  f a
         l
           l

you catch me.
again
and
again.

## SUMMER AIR

the beans are growing,
it's a new year.
dust from the sahara desert
coming in.
a caterpillar in a garden.
a baby's fingers
grasping and clenching
the soil.
where did the time go?

we sit in our chairs,
humming songs.
i cry in that movie,
the way the father
hugs his daughter.
a lonely dirt road.
one song for
the ride home.

JUNE NINETEEN TWENTY-TWENTY

Lord,

thank you for your cotton candy skies and your fields
of flowers and fistfuls of daisies and armloads of hugs
and a brother who picks them for me and a father who
clothes me with his jacket when i am chilly and mem-
ories of that sled and those flowerbeds and that swing-
set, our fake uncle bob and dirt flying on the road, all
while holding a bouquet of your wildflowers. even
though i am slow, you are still growing me. thank you
for delighting in me always.

                                        Amen.

## THE ART OF BEING STILL

there's an art to doing nothing.
strolling around town,
quietly entering a bakery,
biting into an apple tart
at a round table with a window
overlooking the street.
or sitting on an empty bridge
gazing at the sunset with one lone tree,
the bay beneath your feet.
you are flying here
in this space,
and there is nothing
but the breeze to
keep you at peace,
and it is here,
here where the sun dips low
and your back curves,
while your hands steady
the fall,
and you just watch it all,
but somehow
it seems perfect
as the the lesser light begins
to rule over the night.

## TWO NIGHTS AGO, GRANDPA DIED

so unexpected.
like a sunny day
before the storm
that tears the foundation
of your house.

they found him—
grandma did—
pale and sitting
in his chair,
his boots still
on his feet.

both his parents died
about the same.
most likely from heart failure.
and how does it give out
like that?
so unexpected.
nothing you could do.

the thing is,
i never knew how many people
would show up to
bring us food and flowers.
i never expected to hear
all the stories from people
who really *knew* him.
i wonder what
that was like.

but here i am now,
picking up all the other pieces,
the ones not so pleasant,
and trying to figure out where
they fit in my perspective

of him and how to
hold my head high
in front of family and friends who cry
when they miss him.
how i see that picture of us
at great grandma's christmas
where he tries on my headphones,
and i laugh and wonder:
who was this man
to me?

## THE VIEWING WALL

as my dad put it,

"i'm t i r e d
of being put on
d i s p l a y."

# OLD GRANDPA MEMORIES

they're the kind that
i stuffed in a box
and shoved in a shady,
shadowy corner of my basement.
the kind that when
i found them once again,
they were dusty with rips
and smudges and smears
along with stains from termite damage
or too many fingers that
weren't mine holding them,
and now that i have them
in *my* hands,
they are unfamiliar,
unrecognizable.
they're like a book i read
years ago,
and now i can't remember
the order of the words.
there's polaroids,
evidence of his presence.

i hear others' memories of him,
so vivid and clear to them,
but most of mine seem sad and awkward.
the most vivid thing i remember
was that he always asked,
"are you still the fastest in your class?"
the memories
are all so dusty that
you can smell them when
i walk into the room.
i feel either too sad
or not sad enough.
for different reasons,
but i'm trying to convince myself

tears are valid no matter
why they're falling.

so, i'll just keep going through
the basement boxes.
because i don't remember them
the way they're told.
i just see them through a
five, ten, fifteen
year old's eyes.

my fingers carry the dust
for the rest of the day.
and i can't stand
the smell.

## REMEMBER

even in the darkest night,
when you'd wish
you could forget it all,
someday,
you will be thankful.

you'll be thankful
even though your heart
had a hard time
being put back together.
someday, you will be able

to hold your best friend's hand
or hug your daughter
as she goes through it too.
the pain is not a waste.
it never is.

## HERE'S MY DUSTY SURRENDER

Lord,
please water it,
make me grow from ashes.
i'm stuck in a circle;
i don't know which way to go.
i keep ending up
in the same  s p o t.
i want to be found in your grace.
lead my heart there.
the only place
i want to be lost
is in your
e m b r a c e.

you are paving the way.
may i walk
in your footsteps?

# III

## cleaning up after

## A MOMENT IN TIME

window rolled down

my hand sticking out

on a gravel road

bare feet are better for dancing

under the stars

with a watchful moon

driving past houses of stone

people we know and people we don't

new t-swift album

two sets of sisters

last summer night

before school starts.

IN THE HALLWAY

her eyes are saying
the words her lips
cannot form.

she's lost and desperate,
searching and longing,
hungry for love
and to be known.

please see her.
don't just pass her by.
truly and indefinitely
*see* her.

## PRESSED IN FROM ALL SIDES

you slide your thumb
over the tips of your fingers,
lips pressed together.
you're disappointed again.

today,
my friend said
her parents were giving her
the silent treatment.

she told me
it was like a firework
that lit but never went off.
do you risk getting close

in case it blows?

or is it time
to move on?

## STACKED YET SEPARATE

some stories haunt you.
like the way his
coffee-stained eyes
felt soft like rain drops
with a certain terror
hidden inside.

/ / /


sometimes when i'm at
the middle stair landing,
my soul feels separate
from my body, and i do not feel
i belong.

/ / /


some part of me
withered away and
through all the hustling bodies,
i have a clear view
to a window of stacked buildings,
layered with smoke,
and a wispy grey sky
to hold them together.

the world found meaning there
between a window and me.

DISPLAY RACK

in panic,
i searched your eyes
to see if i could find
all the answers
you left behind.
you see,
my heart was open,
on display,
ready to invite yours in.
but when i
searched your eyes,
i could not see
my reflection
staring back at me.
wondering what was wrong,
i checked the display rack,
is everything okay?

s e a r c h i n g,
                                    finding
n o t h i n g.

your heart wasn't yours
to give away.

## TOO HEAVY TO CARRY

i soon became
your dust pan,
cleaning up the mess
you kept sweeping on me.
right when the slate
was clean, and i went
to empty the junk
you left me to carry,
a new pile was
already formed.
you no longer
saw me
in the same light.
just a support
for your brokenness.

now my back is breaking,
and you are becoming
too heavy to carry.
too heavy to hold.

## HOPE ON THE HORIZON

i praise you for the purple skies and full moons.

God is pulling back the blanket
of the dark morning,
and the light is slowly
sneaking through.

today. a new day, an old hope.
Him.
our Savior.

look. the sky
is awakening.

## TARNISHED CORN

as the disappointments
of this world fall on us
like the dry, husky corn
from a lack of moisture,
we know you are good.

i can see the wind
blowing through
those cornfields,
reminding me
you are here.
you chose to walk
on this dusty, dry earth.
all for us.

and the corn grows
because it knows
your voice and
your call.
"how can you be disappointed?!"
the corn exclaims.
"He has given us
everything!"

## THE EXACT TIME

what time was it
when your knees
buckled to the floor
and your heart
succumbed
to the weight
of the world?

your hands used to fit
in the crevices between,
arm and arm,
but now you outgrew
those dusty blue shoes
and moved onto laces
that can't tie themselves.
with each step,
the world grew heavier
on your shoulders
after your arms
could no longer carry.

i wonder what time it was
when you understood that day.

## EARS RINGING

it's a clumsy love,
the kind
you got me
tripping over here,
i'm just falling
to be caught.
take me home,
i'm just waiting
on this park bench
for your call.
take me home.
i don't know
where i am.
the phone stopped ringing.
but now my ears do.
where are you?
i got a heart too heavy
to hold, and i'm worried
you faded like the
morning dew.

## NOVEMBER SEVENTEENTH

when they told me,
something pinched
inside my soul,
twisting it around
like a fork with spaghetti,
and i wanted so badly
to spit it out.

instead,
i threw away
my *extra* gum wrapper,
the promise of it holding
"life's little moments,"
but this was one
i didn't want to chew.
i just wanted to swallow
and let the pain
  pain
     pain
be over and gone and out of
my lungs that haven't been able
to breathe
since.

BURDENED

i walk through
the heavy halls,
endless and
burdensome.

there was a fight
at lunch today.
head pulled back,
seven punches
to the face.
walk away.

brick walls,
they planted a garden
in the fall.
don't they know
the death-like winter
is approaching?

they say he got a two week suspension.
people blame it on a lot of things.
a girl. his family. public schools.
all i see is the
b r o k e n n e s s
of this world.

the flowers are
already wilting
from friday.
heavy and burdened.

## HAPPY DAYS—COME BACK

there's a girl
who once was happy
but dropped it off
on the way to 8th grade
and can't remember
where she lost it.

a girl who analyzes
a hazel, brown clock
in her therapist's room,
wondering if she
ever *was* supposed
to know the 'why' answers
to all those questions.

*where did the*
*sunny days disappear to*
*and why have the*
*gloomy days not gone away?*

she wonders.
she thinks back
to all the possibilities,
but none of it
adds up.

she can still remember
days of happy.
but *why* did they fade?
she can't find the answer.
she doesn't know why
she wakes up
on her bathroom floor,
passed out from so many tears.

is something wrong
with *her?*

or this world
she lives in?
and if the latter,
why won't it
leave her *alone?*

## IT'S TOO LATE NOW

diversions and distractions:
we'll keep running
from the truth
as long as we can
get away.

distant years and depressed times:
no one understands
what we went through—
not even us.

dark days and the devil is prowling:
we can no longer see reality,
only the horror around us,
but it's too late to run,
it's too late to go to anyone,
it's too late now.

we barely missed it
on our evening train ride
every day the last eighteen years.

no one told us
it'd end this way.

## A CLOSED DOOR

just in case you didn't know,
i can still smell
the pieces of decay
and ignorance
you dropped as you left.
there were no consequences
for you. i'm convinced
i was the only one
who carried the baggage.
shakes and theaters,
your arm wrapped around
my shoulder like a
movie scene
as i shrunk into my seat
to fit all of me
inside your arms.

carrying me
was the insistent sound
of keys jangling in your pocket,
unlocking the door to a past
you didn't want to open.
i cracked my soul
and spilled a few scars on the table.
only enough for you
to realize how much depth
i held, and how it
sometimes haunted me.
but the way i dropped
those stones from
my heart at your doorstep
that had a sign saying,
"welcome in,"
but a latch that
was rusted over,
i realized

you never did want me in,
and i was left outside,
talking to a closed door.

## PROVISION IN THIS PLACE

last week,
i worshiped you
for an hour and a half
on the floor.
Jesus, i want more.

i see you in
diagonal clouds,
a tractor surrounded
by cows,
the promise of hay.

Jesus, you are mighty
and great and yet
when your sheep
wander from
their gate,
you search and find them,
like when they put you
to the test.

Lord, you even give the
birds of the sky
a place to rest.

## THIS IS THE MOMENT YOU WERE MADE FOR

the light is dancing
across your room
and darling,
you're a spectacle of wonder
in this place.
a vessel of clay
and morphed to shape
the exact purpose
you will someday fulfill
if you follow
where the Light is guiding.

keep following it.

keep stumbling down
that cobblestone path to find
your true Cornerstone.
keep searching for
the wildflowers that will
lead you to the One
who created all beautiful
and incandescent things.
you were made for this moment.

for this day.

## HANDS RAISED—WE'LL KEEP FIGHTING

but you see
      there is hope
strapped to our fingers,
      words that caught up
      with the paper,
the writer that holds
      the pen that
      translates her heart's content.
the raising of hands
      in the cracks of a church
      too stuffy to breathe,
the rebellious joy
      and the fact that she
      has the choice
to not keep sinking,
      but to keep growing
      amidst the snow falling,
she will be the miracle
      that rises with the sun.

she will keep fighting.

# IV

## finding the lost

# WHAT HAPPENS WHEN OUR HANDS REACH UP

*(joel 2:12-14)*

there's a girl
who's tired and in need
of a rescue.

she raises her hand,
static, alone,
a magnet, a call.

she asks God for help.
she keeps her hand
in the air, and

He reaches down
and takes her from this cage
as long as her hand

is stretched out
toward Him.
and He whispers,

*"i never fail to rescue."*

## A STRUCTURED LIFE I NEVER KNEW
## AND STILL DON'T KNOW IF I WANT

we are each carried
s y s t e m a t i c a l l y
by the code that was
i n s t i l l e d

in us from the time
we were born, and the
p o s t u r e
of our heart changes,

but the
n u a n c e
of our structure
remains the same

even if it is
d e a f e n e d
for a while
by something outside of us.

we run from places
we grew up only to come
wandering back again.
why do we long for
the patterns and nostalgia
of a younger and more innocent
version of ourselves?
back when everything was
good and pure in our eyes.

when asking where we
want to live and plant our feet,
she answered,

*"well, do you want to fill your days*
*with everything new and different*
*or do you want to build something*
*that will last for generations?"*

# THE FJORDS

he was like old leather,
but messy and imperfect,
hair that flopped and eyes
with laughter,
a sky behind them.

the sky of symmetry scattered
along a sweepy horizon and those
were his eyes. he found
his home in the fjords of
a norwegian battlefield, the drifts
of his hair blew overboard, and i scarcely
understood it.

he could fly away at any moment.
his smile was soft and pudgy,
a good deal too nice for anybody, yet
his hands were durable when
the winter snow came
storming in.

then,
it took him away.

he settled among the
scattered skyline with
dreams that fell like drifts
over his forehead, and
we haven't been able
to find him since.

## YEARS OF DESTRUCTION

it all started with
a heart too calloused to care.

years of destruction
turned it hard and twisted
and maybe all those
nail scars had something
to do with it.
but despite the long,
weathering roads,
cracks were formed.

we thought we could
slip through,
to keep going amidst
the dark morning,
but we sunk deeper
into the crevices
we made for ourselves.
no way out
it seemed.
too deep to fix.
maybe start over?

our plan
wasn't working.
we couldn't stop talking
and before we knew
that one calloused heart
turned us all,
and there was no more reality—
no, there were now
craters in our bodies.
we were trapped
and trying to get out.

they say they used
wet fingers to tie
weak ropes, but the thread
slipped through.
they looked in the mirror,
but nothing was ever new.
lost in our minds,
the tornado that came through
could never repair the damage
that broke me too.

## ABORTION

when you can't see the light,
　　　you keep trying to grow
but they cut you down,
　　　they stop you,
they don't like who you are,
　　　they have a plan of their own,
suddenly, you can't breathe,
　　　you can't see the end,
they tell you you're worthless,
　　　they won't let you bend,
they pinch and they pull you,
　　　you're stretching,
still trying to find the light,
　　　the string you're attached to
takes you away like a kite,
　　　you fly higher and
you reach for the stars
　　　you can't see, but they just
beat you down and tell you
　　　what you can and can't be,
you were human,
　　　but they cut you into pieces
because to them, you were just a
　　　mere inconvenience.

## GRATITUDE

thank you Lord.

you provided water

in the middle of a desert.

in the midst of

a lost and broken world,

you provided a Savior.

thank you Lord.

## A BALLAD FOR THOSE WITH BROKEN BODIES

*i'm starting today.*

you head into war
because every time
you look at yourself,
it reminds you
of the fight.
it never
surrenders,
but you just want
a break.

*i failed again.*

you try to pick
yourself up.
you ate your weight
in food again
because the weight
of the world
is crushing you
even here
even now,
and you are trying to find
any way to
breathe again.

*i'm starting now.*

you tell yourself it doesn't matter
what you look like,
that you need to accept
the hips that make your jeans
harder to slip on or
the stomach with creases and folds.
but it keeps telling you

of your failure.
you keep trying to breathe,
but there's no way out
when you're running from
your own body.

*one day at a time.*

each day,
you must choose small steps
because you are on a path
of victory.
the war is now won;
you don't need to keep
fighting anymore.

*i'm free.*

## NOT WHERE THEY SHOULD HAVE ENDED UP

watching my words
f
  a
    l        o
      l      u
                t
of my
mouth
and s o m e r s a u l t i n g
into a
w h i r l p o o l
and spurting into
new ears
where they are heard
in contrast
and s o a k e d
and t r a n s l a t e d
to mean something entirely
different
than how they first

f    e    l    l.

why can't they stop?

## QUIET FARMING TOWN

a fragile pink sky,
highways with endless land, a field filled

                    with flocks of white specks
                    from their endless migration.

legs exposed to the air again,
hearing the sounds of town;

                    a truck driving by,
                    whistling on his route,

birds fighting for space in a tree,
children riding trikes like you used to do,

                    the sweet stage before learning
                    what it takes to control a bike.

take the pedals
and fly away

                    as fast as you can,
                    no turning back.

these children,
they don't know me

                    and yet the crying boy
                    comes up to me,

handing me a stub of chalk
from his tear-filled hand,

                    accusing another of
                    ruining his artwork,

and demanding me to
"draw spongebob."

                    speechless, i get to work.
                    more kids surround,

watching this high schooler
who came to their recess,

                    just for one picture,
                    who is filling their sidewalk

with drawings they all somehow revere.
all too soon, recess is over

                    and they scatter to pick up the pieces.
                    the undeniable trust within these fences.

trees scatter the skyline on my morning drive,
a pond here and there,

                                  a little creek in the ditch,
                                  a tiny town so small

you'll blink and it's gone,
the grain bins and barns

                                  built every once and a while.
                                  watching outside to get their

temperature checked.
the world still isn't

                                  normal, covered faces,
                                  empty spaces, we keep

masking up, moving on.
humans are resilient, you see. we just keep

                                  waking up, keep going.
                                  i felt the breath of Jesus

this morning. it was His
undeniable feeling of calm

                                  and being known beyond
                                  yourself, i want to rest

on this some more.
a girl pauses on

                                  her walk to school,
                                  glancing around at

the breeze, brick walls,
and a tree at the corner.

                                  the wind is so quiet today,
                                  the trees are still,

and the flags don't move.
suddenly, everything is

                                  in perfect pause
                                  like a photograph.

and then a truck drives by,
the steady beat of a quiet farming town

                                  and the melody of children
                                  coming to school.

## A UNIVERSE OF STARS UNSEEN

in a world with
endless sounds,
there is a universe
of stars waiting
to be found,
yet so many eyes
are fixed here with
what is on the ground.

at the end of the day,
it is the person
who keeps reaching
for the stars others can't see
that finds them
when no one else knew
where to start
looking.

# WITHOUT HONESTY: A PART OF ME SUPPRESSED

tightly,
      she slices an apple,
peeling the skin,
      one centimeter,
            then another.
her fingers,
      clutching the knife,
            not knowing what it is
      without it.

some part of me
      has told myself to suppress,
            hide away.
      people don't want honesty.
trying,
      a bird leaves the nest,
            the only place it's ever known,
      flapping wings that reek
            and yet it's beak becomes
                  the wind and shadows and
            the worries were never part
of the design,
      and here it flies
            faster and farther,
      forgetting all it's ever known.

honesty leads to arguments to losing friendships.
i've been hiding so long, i forgot what the real light
looked like. i've been mistaking the dark night
for a bright wave of shining truth and where did i go.
no one sees me. no wait, she says she sees
right through me and somehow that is worse.
panic strikes me, and i'm at a loss for words. i can't hide
behind this curtain, this knife i've clutched.
shaking, i look out a tree i once climbed.
i can't even find what i really feel anymore.

the bird lands on a fence post and sees the seeds
of an apple that once dropped to new soil.
it pecks and gives way to something it
needed all along. and the air
hurts its breast as it sucks up all the life
of a new tree, but it sees the dawn,
and why, the worry is gone.
gone.

it's gone.

## NOSTALGIA x FIVE MILLION

there's an order in life.
like sectioning off
pieces of paper to
make coloring easier.

we just sat in desk chairs,
waiting for the bell.
s i l e n c e.
you don't realize

how much you've changed
until you see the people
around you, and they are
suddenly unrecognizable.

well, you are too.
what happened to
circus performers
holding the door,

teeter totters when
we were young.
pushed on a swing
too big for you,

chalk on sidewalks,
trace your hand,
and it's a turkey.
now, you sit on

park benches
waiting for the
door to be unlocked.
contacts out your eyes,

hey i got the job,
life is speeding up
and slowing down.
all your classes

spin your head until
you go to the bathroom stall,
take off your mask,
and finally

b r e a t h e.

the moments you thought
you were enjoying are
swiftly passing by.
let's roll down the hills,

shall we?
geese fly overhead and
you remember your
younger self looking

up to the sky
in hopes someday
you'd learn to fly
but on the way,

you stumbled and tripped,
fell and lost in
the race you had to win.
doors are closed,

you are blind again
to the world you
thought you knew,
but it turned its

back on you.
when will dandelions
come back again?
i need a wish.

## STREAMS IN THE WASTELAND

*(isaiah 43:18-19)*

taking a step into the void and
unsure if there will be a place
for my foot to land on the
other side.

would i be letting fear control me
if i truly trusted Him?
i conform so easily
to those around me
but if my friends
are dying of starvation,
i don't want to give in too—
rather, may i feed them
your food from heaven.
i want to risk the wreck
and everything falling apart
in order to be closer
to Jesus.

i want to follow Him
with no guarantees of safety.
i'm tired of everything
being handed to me
and living in hypocrisy.
if what i'm saying i
believe is true,
shouldn't i be
living for it?
i'm s t e p p i n g
into the
u n k n o w n.
i've exhausted all
other options.

God, i want to be
at the end of my rope,
pull me out of the water.
this right here,
this is proof that
you don't leave me
gasping for air.

Lord, i'm ready to move.
take me there.
cut down the walls,
the borders,
the limitations
i build in my heart.
i don't want to stay in the grave and claim
to know your name. no,
you didn't stay in the grave.

Jesus, may i step out
of the boat on your command,
and if my feet start to sink,
would you reach out your hand.
as i wander in the driest desert,
make a stream in my wasteland.

# V

## coming back home

## A BLANK POEM: UNWRITTEN

it's the first blank
poem, and i don't know
where to start.
so i guess,
i should start with what
i see.

outside, a cloud-wave
rolls in and birds fly
to trees in pairs.

a note a few days ago said
i was passing cars on sunlit highways
so bright i couldn't see the lines.

and a day later, fairy clouds glide
across a blue majestic sky into a vast sea,
and maybe it's the clouds and ocean that speak

daily to me, but i see
my God in all of this creation.
there is no blank poem that

He hasn't already written.

## I SAW A NEW PAIN TODAY

from where i'm sitting,
the world just got
a little heavier.
like the heavy that hurts
but you're also grateful
people aren't hiding
in shadows and
staying in the shallows
any longer.

heavy like a guy
reaching out to me
and asking how to pray.

heavy like a girl
telling me how my words
were what she needed to hear
this morning after
waking up numb.

heavy like a little boy
telling me his parents split,
and he misses his dad.
holding up a toy car,
he says this is what
he remembers
him by.

"i wish they were still together
but now they're happier apart."
and it broke my heart
to see a world where
he and his little sister
were split in two from
the time they were young.

racing toy cars down a hill
isn't the same when
that car reminds you of
the father who left.

heavy got a little heavier today.

## PLAYHOUSE FULL OF SCRIBBLES

somewhere long ago
was a little girl with
uneven bangs who drank from
an empty teapot
and wrote
scribbles as words
because her hands could not
yet form the letters
her heart
was dying to read.
to see. to feel.

today, i write for
that little girl who made
w's and m's
over and over again,
willing there
to be something.
anything. there to say.
there to be.
to see. to feel.

her words are here.
the girl she is now
only has fourteen more days
left of high school.
her whole world is
before her, but
she can't help feeling like
that girl with uneven bangs
and a bunny smile
in a playhouse full
of scribbles.

and yet, she misses
her shy innocence
all the same.
someday, she'll look back
and see the scribbles of today,
where they took her,
where they've been.
how they helped her
to see. to feel.

she is writing now.

## AUNT VERNA

i look into her 101-year-old eyes,
black craters on a raisin
wrinkled face with
plastered pink lips.
it was hard to see,
to picture who
she once was.
but she knew
who i was.

she *knew* as she
looked in my eyes.
it was as if she
knew who i'd be
even after she
was gone.

and i didn't know if this was
the last time i'd see her,
even with all the life hidden
in her eyes, her days were
coming to a close,
but i promised her i'd write.

i'd keep on writing.

## HIGH SCHOOL UNPLUGGED MY BATHTUB

she was the needle
stuck in my vein,
sucking out my blood that
wasn't hers to take.
but i let her have it.
i gave it away.

he was the summer heat
that killed my new growth,
scorching any joy that overflowed
and letting it wilt away
with the tumbleweeds.

they were flies,
landing on my back,
held up by lies.
i shooed them away,
but after a while,
i let them stay.

somewhere it was sucked out of me
and poured down the drain.
somewhere, something
unplugged my bathtub,
and i've been naked in the corner
ever since.

# WHAT THE FUTURE HOLDS

someday,
i won't wake up here
anymore.

someday,
i'll be laying in my dorm
room, thoughts of the future
flitting across a window
or down my face.

someday,
there will be more stretch
marks, more wrinkles,
more babies to hold, more
lips to kiss.

someday,
i'll sit back on a
porch swing and watch my
grandchildren grow up.

someday,
there will be more laughter
in these halls that isn't from me,
but i'll be listening, and i'll be
reminded of this old book.

someday,
i won't wake up here
anymore.

## DANDELION PICKERS

broken fences, dirt fields, russ's muffler repair.
scraggly green trees and creeks with bridges.
gas pumps that don't work,
an unused railroad, a cemetery
behind a school, as if learning leads to death,
and sometimes i think we set them up
for future failures rather
than success. grain bins and patches of weeds
the farmers hate but the children love to pick
and hand to the farmers saying,
"look, i found you a flower."
the forbidden flower. the thing you never understand.
dandelions are only beautiful to five year old eyes.
we never understood our home.
until it was almost gone.

## SKYLINE

i wonder how much sky
we can see with our eyes.
it's beyond what we even
imagine it to be.
how does our depth perception
change from when we
go up to when we're
walking on the ground?
how do we know
our role when the
sky looks so big
from down here,
but when we fly,
we only see the clouds?

## ONE FOOT. ANOTHER.

we were brightly lit streets,
you and i,
causing up a storm.
and most days
they pronounced
our names wrong
but we were gonna
keep marching
until we saw the dawn.

# LIFE FLASHED BEFORE MY EYES

a kid ran out
in the street today.
a car slammed
on its breaks.

seconds before,
the kid emptied
his shoes of rocks
from the playground.

minutes before,
he was skipping on
the sidewalk
playing abra cadabra
and invisible backflips.

an hour before,
he picked two girls
dandelions and told them
to blow because then
they looked like snow
and tickled his nose.

a kid ran out
in the street today.
a car slammed
on its breaks.

it just missed him.
he's okay.
empty shoes.
a skip in his step.
dandelion wishes
on his fingertips.

he's okay.

## A DARK STAIRWELL

soft.
the music blows
into her ears and

swoosh.
she brings her hands
up to her face with

sobs.
they seep out of her,
and finally she is letting go of

sails.
she is moving down a sea with waves
no one else can see, and she is

scared.
she covers her eyes and holds onto the rail
as she feels her way up the stairs in the dark but

stop.
arms wrap around her. this embrace is the home
she was sent to. the home where she always wanted to be.

WONDERING...

how

    can

        i

    love

  you

better?

## IT'S THE LITTLE THINGS

target bags and hugs on a
living room floor where our
mattresses cover and rainbows
touch the door,
you've never seen before
how breathtaking the sky is
or how the pen draws creation,
or a birthday cake,
layered and flowered
in celebration of
nineteen years and turning,
needles bleed out threads of beauty
outputting embroidered bags,
and a facetime call from my brother,
only shows the top of his head,
and i'm laughing because i forget
the wonder in early mornings,
chipped nail polish, dark polaroids,
white feet, movie stubs, sensitive skin,
and detailed lines, so intricate
the words on the page and
the sunshine smile on her lips,
i feel the nearness of God
in my hair, on my arm,
within my fingertips.
it's the little things.

## NURSERY RHYMES

sleepy children tug
on their mamas and
blankets are reluctant
to leave their hands.
balancing babies on hips
and making up stories as
they sit in a circle,
their hands dance to ring around
the rosie, and they don't know
most nursery rhymes carry
pasts of evil and next comes
london bridges falling down
and then they lay on their cots
and dream of when their mamas
will come to pick them up.
their eyelashes flutter,
and they coo in their sleep.

## SHE STOPPED OPENING THE DOOR

the hands of her father
caused her to falter
and lose any hope
for men to change,
to be better.
all men, it seemed,
could do nothing
to please her,
she needed a dreamer,
but came back with
a fever that got to
her head.
they never changed,
they were all liars.
she couldn't let them in.
she'd never let them in.
she couldn't let herself in.

she stopped opening the door.

## WHAT WE FOUND OUT

twenty-two years ago,
after the gunman
emptied the cry
of his weapon,
it snowed in
a little nebraska
town.

they say april showers
bring may flowers,
but april snow settled in
and churned our comforts
cold. what is life without that
constant fluttering
in your stomach?

you see what i mean?
it came out of nowhere
and settled on something
that wasn't supposed to be.
i found fear
as a friend
through these years.

only because without it
was a numbness
i was too scared
to carry.
lacking nothing,
needing everything,
words mixed up,
i want to start over,
i need to begin
again, only the world
doesn't offer any
promises truly.

the alcoholic still finds
his drink after years
of turning away.
the man who promised
faithfulness still
cheats on his tests. and yet,
i hear a whisper, an
alarm of hope in a

voice not easily heard
unless you reach the end
of yourself
and acknowledge the
snow that came
and wasn't supposed
to be, and He
says to you,
     *child,*
      *i make you new.*

the voice offers
a promise the world
could never keep.
it whispers,

     *don't die trying to find*
     *favor with fear. don't run*
     *when the mistakes plague*
     *what you hold dear.*
     *i am here now and that's*
     *all you need.*

shots ran out,
and the last words
to escape her mouth were:

"you know i do."

and everything became right.

right now.

## I ALWAYS WANTED TO GROW UP

it was that pink toy cadillac
that got me in the driver's seat
for the very first time.

                                    i had a malt today.
                    it reminded me of summer camp
                                    in sixth grade.


the fewer days between
now and moving out,
i feel more distance

                        grow between us, and i try to
                    fight it, but sister, i am so sorry
                            i have to leave you.


growing up, i discovered
the world expects a lot of you,
that dreams don't always

                                    come true,
                        and that dandelions
                            are weeds too.


i never knew that growing up
meant being the girl waiting
in the parking lot by herself

                                for a friend.
                    not risking going
                        inside because


anxiety reigns on the ground
she walks, and she prays in her car
for it to stop.

## CREATED TO CREATE

our hands carry the dust
on our fingertips
that came from
our past. and we hold
it here in the field,
as we bake bread,
our hands do these things,
but they are really
individually created
to create.

we hold the pen
between our fingers
and flesh out a story
of the things we've touched,
the things we've held.
she swung from monkey bars once,
and her fingers slipped.
she held on tight after that.

# THE FINGERPRINT OF THE IMMIGRANT

i opened my eyes
and saw humanity for the first time.
it was in the
                  f i n g e r p r i n t
on the wall, all those
verses tied together, oh so small,
they hold a piece of you
you never realized would come through
until those old jean shorts,
that record player,
and the empty promises like a shuffled
             d e c k  o f  c a r d s,
you never knew
what you would draw, what it would
mean, and where you'd go from there,
but i'll give you a start.

it's here, in the hugs of the
                  i m m i g r a n t s
who started this story
for us. this place we want to
disown was first held by people
who were
            d i s o w n e d
from their homes, and now we're
trying to do the same thing back?

to tell the truth, i see that postcard,
that broken back, the ache
of another day in a field full
of livelihood, of a place your family
calls home.

and yet,
sometimes i'm so worried life will go
             f a s t e r

than i can catch up, and i'll be
of the same mind i am now when
i die, but i forget how much
i soak in, how much i learn
in only one day
that in 60 or 70 something years
i will surely know much more than i know
            as i write this.

and i never told you, but it wasn't me
who pulled myself out of that pit.
no, in the darkness,
there's an immigrant
i called out to,
one who was disowned
for a while, being held by my
disgusting past, holding up a crown of
my deceit on His head.

His name is Jesus. and i am
            u n a s h a m e d
of what He did because i know
that when i pick from that
deck, it won't be by chance.
it will be by purpose.

and i know it won't be
an empty promise because
            He already saved me
when i was drowning. no, here

in the silence, i talk to Him,
and this immigrant listens because
He knows this place will
disown me. it does everyday.

He knows i am the immigrant
born in uncharted waters and that

His arms in heaven are where
i will finally
make my home.

## MAKE ME A WILDFLOWER

Lord,
make a wildflower
out of me.

i want to dance in
the wind whether they're
watching or not.
i want to grow despite
being asked to.
i want to live in faith,
not fear,
that you will provide for me
and help me to fulfill
the purpose you've created me for.

Lord,
make a wildflower
out of me.

## JUNE FIFTH: UNSCRIPTED THOUGHTS

it's like you're giving me permission to step out, to
speak about my faith. you're not finished with me.
you're saying that you will still lead me because you
died for me and you love me and you leave the 99 for
me and when i read that verse about the shepherd dy-
ing for his sheep, i first thought why? for such stupid,
useless sheep, and then i realized they were me, and you
gave your life for my stupid, useless soul and how can i
not praise you right here on this bathroom floor?
hallelujah, thank you Jesus.

*(john 10:11)*

# A DOOR

it started with a barbed wire fence
and ungloved hands gripping it
so tight the blood stained the grass.

it was the only way through.

suddenly, a bridge was formed
connecting something that wasn't now
into a maybe.

maybe they would cross the bridge.

love doesn't start with hugs. it starts
with a smile, with sitting at a lonely lunch table
despite judgmental stares.

it starts here.

a bridge, a possibility, stepping stones
to a shore that reaches an ocean and from there,
a door.

it's so simple.
too simple really.
but you just knock.

yes, you knock.

because once you get there,
it is a guarantee that the One on the
other side is waiting to open it

for you.

so, just knock.
you've made it this far, passed
the barbed wire fence and bridge of possibility.

now, here it is.

the door you've been waiting for.
just wait, wait for that sound of the hinges creaking
and a door wide open

for you to enter in.

## FORGOT THE PEPPER

it's the mornings
poetry comes
to your pen.
your father makes
breakfast,
delivered,
eggs, he forgets
to add the pepper.
you want a new
beginning, and
it's offered with
open arms.

Jesus, today,
will you hold me
a little bit
longer?

RIPTIDES, SWATHER WINDOWS,
& A LACK OF OXYGEN

I.
red flags.
two going up.
it's a riptide,
they say,
stay on the beach
the waves aren't where
you wanna be.
people get swept under.

a man once valiantly formed
a human chain to help all those
who ignored the flags
and their warning of no going back.

riptides, they sweep
you under, breathless,
can't fight them,
swim out to sea
to escape death,
closer to sand, and they'll
take you forever.
this man, with the weight
of his hands, held on
and only when they were all
back to shore, did he wash up
on the beach,
laid in the sand,
and took his last breath.


II.
sitting on the ground
of the swather.
it's probably '06 although

132

i've been coming here
since i was an infant.
playing with pliers,
pretending they're fish.
leaning my head on the glass,
falling asleep, *bang!*
the bumps hit my forehead,
jolt, look and see
dad laugh quietly,
ask if i'm okay.

fast forward now,
it's my little brother
behind the wheel,
i'm in the passenger seat.
not as small as i once was,
shoulders squeeze in between
the door and his handle,
my forehead still hits
the glass.
                    *beep beep.*
i wake up, and it's
grown dark.
"still here?"

"yeah,"
he says.

III.
they took dad to
the hospital.
lack of oxygen.
if covid don't kill ya,
separation will.
he cried when the ambulance
came to transfer him, and he
could finally see his wife.

machines, *beep,*
he can barely stand,
oxygen levels drop, ICU,
a daughter who can't look
at him, for the tears threaten
to never stop.
she sits at home,
staring out the window,
a white truck pulls in,
but it's not him.
eating alone,
he isn't coming home.
not tonight.

staying up late,
waiting for her brother
to come in.
the stars are out.
her mom spends the days
in the hospital with him.
he's finally getting better,
she says.
his daughter,
in the dark of the dim
living room light,
feels like that little girl
bumping her head,
but when she looks over
to see him sitting there,
the chair is empty,
and she cries out
"daddy!" into the
nonsense air.

the riptide pulls her under,
there's no place left to swim,
no human chain,
no more grasping

for a sandy beach
or an unmarked
mind grave.

"he'll be home tomorrow,"
her mother says.

## THE MESSAGE YOU FOUND

we write the languages we speak,
not necessarily what
we believe.
it's hard to put words
to paper. sometimes what you find
isn't what you were looking for.

exposure in words is
tissue on bone, and
you shouldn't see it
but sometimes you do and
isn't that a poet's job?
to expose a part

people can't naturally see?
to reveal something only words
can make them believe?
it's messy, and sometimes the mess
carries over to the one whose
eyes scan the lines

and look for the truth they
wanted to hear but not what
they needed to hear. you want an excuse?
look somewhere else.
because excuses are just
private property, no trespassing signs:

eventually someone someday
will venture past the line you drew,
and you'll have to explain
to the other side of you,
you never wanted to, and the exposure
came and ripped your tongue

right out of your mouth.
we all stand naked, arms
s t r e t c h e d   o u t
waiting for a bullet that
never actually comes
because this exposure

poets write about is often the thing
that makes the gunman put his weapon down
and stand side by side with us. it is
not vain to let your hair down sometimes.
i'm not here to hold you back.
i'm just writing to show you

there's more to the message
than what they say about you.
for you.
to you.
you.
u.

UNFINISHED YET WHOLE

they told me i write
beautifully,
but i just can't
put down the pen.

it's summertime now,
and i'm expected to finish
my time here,
but am i ever really done?

for a long time i worried
i was. done. finished.
that's it, you know?
but He told me i wasn't.

He told me i'm just
unfinished and that it's
okay to let the pen linger
a little longer if i still

have words to say.
so i keep writing, because for now
i'm not done.
i'm still putting pen to paper.

and yet, He whispers,
*you are whole.*
so i am complete?
i am completely unfinished,

and *yet*
i am perfectly whole.
my soul has found the One
it loves, and now i write

not to find the part of me
left to discover because
He *knows* that me already.
no, instead,

i wrap up this story
He's written through me,
and it's okay if it's messy
or the ink spilled and smeared.

it's okay because
He's got more plans for me.
*try again,*
He whispers.

so i hold this life loosely,
and let His words write through me
because i finally see myself as He sees me
and that is i am

*unfinished yet whole.*

COLLEGE IS

college is
hair flying out an
open window on a
sunset drive to
the mountains.

college is
swing dancing,
or rather, learning how to
with complete strangers,
the lifts and tricks stealing
your breath, and you're
caught up in a moment
of twirling.

college is
a lonely couch on a
monday night when anxiety found you,
and the sofa is too soft for it,
so the floor is all
that will hold you as
you splay yourself out,
waiting to be found.

college is
polaroid pictures,
dates and people who
found you in that
moment you stole
and taped it on your wall.

college is
a trash can waiting
to be emptied,
full of last week's discarded
coffee filters and leftovers

leading you nowhere,
you're finding it hard
to fill yourself
anymore.

college is
a loud hallway
with nerf gun wars
and movies and laughing
while studying and
chopsticks falling
out of your hair
as you race down it.

college is
a lonely guitar
waiting to be strummed,
but then for an hour,
it gets pulled out
of its case and played
for a room full
of souls dying
for change.

college is
running a pen down
to no ink to catch
all your fleeting thoughts
and holding onto those
quarters you don't
want to spend.

college is
your roommate spinning around
because her mind is
blank, and she screams
into some void
of silence,

confused, she ponders
over a metaphor
and finds her days
filled with the formative
when she longs for
the creative, and sometimes
indonesia falls on
her heart, the place
she grew up beyond
the borders of colorado, and now
she eats yuzu chicken soba,
cries out into an empty space,
"yes! this is what
i've been missing!"

that's what
college is.

NEAR

Lord, i long for your
sweet counsel.
the kind that asks
me to come,
walk on water toward you.
you knew, though,
before i stepped out of
that vessel
i would sink,
start to drown in what
i felt was reality,
when in actuality,
your hand was always
there, ready to pull
me back up.
Lord, thank you
for being near.

MY BEAUTIFUL LITTLE LIFE—
AND IT ISN'T EVEN MINE

as i sit back
and analyze my
beautiful
little life,
i have seen
all the places,
those jumbled up spaces,
where God has shown up
the most. you know,
those terrifying times
where you can't move,
fear grabbed you by
the neck, and the blood is stuck.
the guilt, it held you down
and stuck a target on
your back, endlessly being found.

but He came rushing in,
fighting for my
breath. it was a
turn of events
the day i realized
shame was not a scar
i was continually
trying to avoid.
no, God allowed it
to be a bruise,
black and ugly for a time,
but now healed by His
loving arms of grace,
and i didn't deserve it.
the way He loves,
it is only a mystery.
one the detectives
couldn't even solve.

one the world tries to ignore.
but they can't deny my story,
no, not anymore.

it's out there.
with these sentences.
these punctuation
marks.
these spaces.
i'll never fully
comprehend.
so instead,
with these words i'll just
give Him praise.
i mean, He gave me
the words in
the first place.
they aren't mine.
neither is this story.
it's all His.

i'm
all His.

# ACKNOWLEDGEMENTS

First of all, I want to acknowledge how grateful I am for all of you who followed along through this entire journey. Thank you from the bottom of my heart for holding these words so tenderly in your hands. I pray you felt the presence of Jesus.

Next, I just want to thank every person whose story made it into this book or who inspired me to write any of these poems. The painful stories impacted me just as much as the joyful ones, and I am grateful for them all.

A big thank you and shout out to my absolutely impeccable roommate and artist, Kailyn! This book is a reality because you came alongside me in my discouragement and, with your creative fingers, helped make my vision come true. Your consistent support is the reason this work is finally finished. You. Are. Incredible. Love you, Klinny!

Thank you to both of my phenomenal English teachers; Cindy Myers, for noticing how long I let my pen linger on the paper and then giving me the space to keep writing, and Laura Bloss, for opening up new worlds to me through words of all kinds: spoken, written, and performed. I am grateful for the courage you both gave me to write.

Thank you, mom and dad, for raising a daughter who loved books and writing even when you didn't understand where I got it from. Thank you for encouraging me and inspiring me and for anxiously waiting all these years to read my work. Your support and love mean everything to me.

Thank you, Tyler, for hyping me up as my little brother. You're growing up too fast. I hope this book motivates you to get off your video games and read something...and maybe write something too.

Larissa, I am so glad I had you as a sister all these years. You always let me tell you about my next great story idea or explain my strenuous writing process. Thank you for never getting tired of me and continuing to support me.

Thank you, Holly, for listening to my dreams for this book and emboldening me to pursue them. Paulina, thank you for helping me discover more about the

146

joy and intimacy of Jesus and for inspiring me to not give up when I was seriously considering it. Thank you, Nana, for making me write a poem every Thanksgiving, Christmas, and Easter when I came over. None of those actually made it into this book, but you pushing me to "write something" without any concrete inspiration helped me during all the wicked writing slumps.

To everyone who said they'd be the first to buy a copy of this book, I know you couldn't all be the first in reality, but to me, you were. Also, a big shoutout to everyone who helped develop me as a writer by offering to read my work, sending me a book, or encouraging me in any way. THANK YOU A MILLION TIMES AND MORE to all of you! You have a special place in my heart.

And thank you to my Father in Heaven and Savior, Jesus Christ, who is the real inspiration for this book. Without You, I could not write, nor would I be able to say that I am unfinished yet whole. You have guided me on this entire journey, given me grace, picked me back up again, and held me close. I am grateful for a life that is not mine, but totally Yours.

*Photo by Jessie Boyle*

Reyana Joy is a 19 year old writer who was raised on a farm in a little corner of Nebraska. She has been writing since before she can remember, but she discovered poetry as the perfect release she needed during her last few years of high school. Reyana has been passionate about sharing her faith since learning of the captivating nearness and love of Jesus in her life. Today, she hopes to give Him glory in all that she does and to encourage others through her words. Reyana's next adventure is attending Colorado Christian University to study Secondary English Education in hopes of one day inspiring students to express and discover themselves through words. This is her first book.

CPSIA information can be obtained
at www.ICGtesting.com
Printed in the USA
BVHW031758130222
628919BV00007B/194